IN A CITY WHERE THE SPIRIT AND LEGACY OF MIES VAN DER ROHE LIVE ON,
Krueck & Sexton Architects has made its mark with designs that draw from classic modernism as well as from the current architectural discourse. As Franz Schulze writes in the introduction, the firm has been inspired "to reexamine the canon and open it to a variety of avenues hitherto unimagined."

Ron Krueck and Mark Sexton have worked together since 1980. Both partners studied at the Illinois Institute of Technology, and their work is characterized by an exploration of modernism and its possibilities in the late twentieth century. In addition, perhaps due to Krueck's studies at the Art Institute of Chicago, the practice incorporates an understanding of modern art and how its methods might be applied to architecture.

The sixteen projects presented in this volume are documented with remarkable color photographs and meticulous presentation drawings, as well as evocative graphic and painterly representations of the spaces created. Krueck and Sexton's commentary on each work discusses its progression from commission to completed work, and also traces the evolution of their visual language.

Among the residential works shown are the masterful Steel and Glass House, the expressive Painted Apartment, and the spectacular Stainless Steel Apartment high above Lake Shore Drive. Also included are larger-scale buildings, with completed works such as two projects for Hewitt Associates and competition entries for the Arts Club of Chicago and the Amerika-Gedenkbibliothek in Berlin. The exceptional body of work clearly portrays an approach to design that is strong and sensible, yet ambitious and sensuous.

Work in Progress, a new series, brings the work of prominent members of the emerging generation of architects and designers to the forefront. Each volume presents its subject through built and unbuilt projects thoroughly illustrated with a variety of visual material. The engaging format and proactive editorial voice invite the reader to participate in the current cross-cultural and inter-disciplinary thinking that defines the design profession today.

Franz Schulze, professor of art history at Lake Forest College in Illinois, is the author of **Mies van der Rohe: A Critical Biography** and **Philip Johnson: Life and Work.** He is also the editor of **The Mies van der Rohe Archive at the Museum of Modern Art,** a fourteen-volume catalogue raisonné published in 1993. He is currently working on a book about Mies's Farnsworth House.

RON KRUECK   MARK SEXTON

WORK IN PROGRESS

KRUECK SEXTON

ARCHITECTS

INTRODUCTION BY Franz Schulze

THE MONACELLI PRESS

First published in the United States of America in 1997 by
The Monacelli Press, Inc.
10 East 92nd Street, New York, New York 10128.

Copyright © 1997 The Monacelli Press, Inc.

Library of Congress Cataloging-in-Publication Data
Krueck & Sexton : architects / introduction by Franz Schulze.
p. cm. — (Work in progress series)
Includes bibliographical references.
ISBN 1-885254-53-9
1. Krueck & Sexton Architects. 2. International style (Architecture)—Influence.
I. Series: Work in progress (New York, N.Y.)
NA737.K77K78 1997
720'.92'2—dc21   97-5775

Printed and bound in Hong Kong

Designed by Rick Valicenti & chester at THIRST
Compiled by Timothy Tracey
Edited by Andrea E. Monfried

We wish to acknowledge the spirit and vision of A. James Speyer,

and the participation in our work by the architects:
Bill Callahan, John Carhart, Russell Castle, Frank Cavanaugh,
Chun Cham, Carolyn Corogan, Martin Dahl, Paul Danna,
Ursula Dayenian, Tod Desmarias, Edward Donnely, Rich Drozd,
John Ekholm, Rob Falconer, Perry Janke, Robin Johnson, Amy Jordan,
Winston Koh, Kit Krankel, Keith Lasko, Miles Lindblad,
William Mahalko, Andrea Mason, Lucinda Mellott, Fred Norris,
Drew Ranieri, Michael Robinson, John Ronan, Noberto Rosenstein,
Patricia Schroettner, Thomas Shafer, Alex Sims, Susan Stevens,
Hans Thummel, Timothy Tracey, Don Wetzel, Edward Witkowski, and
James Zeigler

and especially the encouragement of Anstiss Hammond Krueck and
Katherine Bajor Sexton.

The failure of postmodernism to carry
through a full-scale revolution in
architecture has had the effect, ironically,
of encouraging the revitalization of
the very tradition it sought to overthrow.
Yet if modernism has enjoyed new life
during the past generation, it is not due
to an uncritical return to the canon.
Instead, a pluralist climate stirred to
some degree by postmodernism itself has
inspired a brace of younger architects
to reexamine the canon and open it to a variety of avenues hitherto unimagined.

Among the most challenging of these latter-day designers are partners Ron Krueck and Mark Sexton, whose accomplishment is all the more arresting because it has occurred in that bastion of orthodox modernism, Chicago. That city was ruled by the magisterial Mies van der Rohe not only during the thirty years he spent there after his immigration from Germany in 1938, but in the decades subsequent to his death. No less striking, both Krueck and Sexton freely acknowledge their debt to Mies and to the curriculum he fashioned and oversaw at their alma mater (where Krueck is now a professor), the Illinois Institute of Technology.

Chicago figures further in the equation, although in ways, reflective of pluralism, that complicate the matter before they clarify it. Krueck also spent a portion of his early years as a student of painting at the School of the Art Institute, where a Chicago tradition of a quite different kind has long been sustained by a faculty whose idiosyncratic approach to the making of art has been almost diametrically opposed to **modernist rationalism.** Moreover, even as he and Sexton learned Miesian fundamentals at IIT, they learned something from other teachers there as well, who though conversant with the orthodoxy, remained marginal to it. Thomas Beeby, for one, a graduate of the Cornell University School of Architecture, was instrumental in helping them to know the writings of Cornell's reigning theoretician, Colin Rowe.

The earliest major efforts of the Krueck & Sexton office point principally, though not exclusively, to Mies. Allusion to the master's favored materials is evident in the very name of the Steel and Glass House, a work from 1981 that bears out a further influence in its unyielding rectilinearity and the two-to-three rhythm of the bays on the street facade. A brick wall that extends part of the way along the front, necessitating a jog in any path to the entrance, recalls similar usages in the residential designs of Mies's German career, while the prominently inverted pier between the second and third bays brings to mind a famous device associated with his American years, the recessed corner of the classroom buildings at IIT.

The plan and the organization of the interior of the Steel and Glass House provide the chief evidence of a form that comes closest to functioning as the seminal component of the Krueck & Sexton architectural **vocabulary: the rectangle.** Two rectangular arms are joined — more exactly, fitted — to a single larger rectangular tract; the three together comprise yet another, still larger rectangle in an interweave that occurs in both plan and elevation. A shape readily associated with Mies, the rectangle is asserted with comparable force in the composition of the interior. Yet the main living space is two stories high, a treatment foreign to Mies (the sole exception being his unrealized design for the Library and Administration Building at IIT), but distinctly reminiscent of Le Corbusier and, in the glass brick surrounding the circular stair, of Pierre Chareau's 1928–30 Maison de Verre in Paris. The most compelling single feature of the living area is a great rectangular plane that serves as both a wall and the ground for a mural, with that double identity bearing out the Krueck & Sexton claim that it is not only functional, a divider of spaces, but expressive, a veritable abstraction of space.

A similar multiplicity of roles is imposed on the rectangle in later works, with the designers relating their objectives to lessons drawn from modern painting as well as from modern architecture. The **plan libre** of the Thonet Showroom of 1982 is organized by vertical layers of perforated screens that owe their texture and varied colors to the surfaces of neo-Impressionist pointillist art. The Painted Apartment, completed in 1983, repeats this treatment, with an added, almost shocking abandonment of the ninety-degree angle in favor of a dizzying curvilinearity of surfaces. The rectangles that form the walls have been warped as well as perforated, so that the plan seems a maze of veils of transparent convexities and concavities. Transparency, in fact, is a key quality here, the "literal" sort that Colin Rowe, in his essay "Transparency: Literal and Phenomenal," defines as pervious by the virtue of the physical character of the materials used to achieve it.

But Krueck and Sexton are no less taken by Rowe's "phenomenal" transparency. "When we read," Rowe offers, ". . . of 'transparent overlapping planes' we sense that more than physical transparency is involved." Rowe finds this "phenomenal" transparency in the massing of Le Corbusier's Villa Stein, and it is equally apparent in the frequent overlay of rectangles in Krueck & Sexton's work, whether in twisted, curvilinear aspect, as in the Painted Apartment, or confined to stricter planar geometry, as in the interior of the so-called Brick and Glass House of 1996.

This last effort is as late as the Painted Apartment is early. Betweentimes Krueck and Sexton have roamed through an adventurous assortment of straight and bent partitions, single and multiple elevations, and formal and informal plans, depending most often on examples learned from Mies or Le Corbusier, but nearly as frequently and with no less a will on the ordered cubism of Braque and Picasso or the wandering dadaist constructions of Kurt Schwitters. The result has been a remarkable form of mannerist modernism, or as the two Chicagoans expressed it in a recent interview,
        "the classical simple sentence turned into a complex sentence,
    reliant nonetheless on the same principles of grammar."

RON KRUECK   MARK SEXTON

Our office was formed by an encounter with a young collector who wanted a house that would look like a factory on the outside and Milan 1970 on the inside. This first work was willfully minimal in an attempt to focus successfully on the manipulation of the basic architectural elements: space, structure, proportion, color, and material.

While attempting to maximize light and privacy for this two-story glass house in the city, a U-shaped plan evolved that took advantage of the sixty-six feet of frontage while creating an entrance plaza, center court, and informal rear yard. Though this U-shaped plan worked well functionally, visually we thought it was too baroque a form. A rigorous analysis of the plan dissolved the U into three rectilinear components that were then reintegrated into a single rectangle.

This rectangle is set fifteen feet behind the building line of the street, which is defined by high brick garden walls aligned with the facades of adjacent buildings. Thus the residence is simultaneously contextual and an interruption in the line of brick-clad houses of the neighborhood. The plan required the rotation and abutting of three separate structural systems, which allows for an expression of the frame and skin on the front and rear elevations. The detailing and expression of the rotated and abutted condition permit the famous Mies inverted corner to occur at the three-fifths point of the entrance elevation, which coincides with the change in direction of the steel angle frames. Entrance panels of steel subway grating are treated as a skin and pushed out of plane with the rest of the facade.

Inside, the ceiling heights on the first floor reinforce an understanding of the plan as two long legs with a connection in the center, while the double-height ceiling of the living pavilion inverts the composition and ties the initial two legs back together. The wall of the living room is pulled back and severed from the rest of the block, to be read as the edge of yet another rectangle. This rectangle connects living room and courtyard and is further reinforced by notches in the opposing garden wall. The terrazzo floor slides outside and creates a rectangle of paving that extends from the entrance through the court and to the rear yard. Its relationship to the garden walls establishes the fact that the plan is not limited to the fluctuations within the house, but that the visual forces are extended to the perimeter of the site, the original rectangle, where they are brought back into resolution.

As the three independent structures were integrated and articulated in plan, we addressed similar concerns in elevation by the introduction of a reveal of light, which traces the rear elevation, crosses the roof, and descends the front elevation, returning back into the house as its entry. Passing through this reveal of light is the first time one experiences the interior space; this is part of a sequence of six turns needed to reach the central living space. Clarifying the three primary rectangles by this reveal also initiates an important nighttime elevation: an elaborate composition of light. Functional elements, which act as spaceless volumes of pinks, yellows, and blues, are freely interjected into the space and are in clear juxtaposition to the rigid glass curtain wall.

The offset wall in the living room became a focal point at the end of the project. We devised a mural, not executed, by superimposing the implied grids of the structure and window wall with other elements of the space. A synthesis was achieved by completing some elements as required and erasing others that had already been projected into the space. The mural and the space would have become absolutely interdependent.

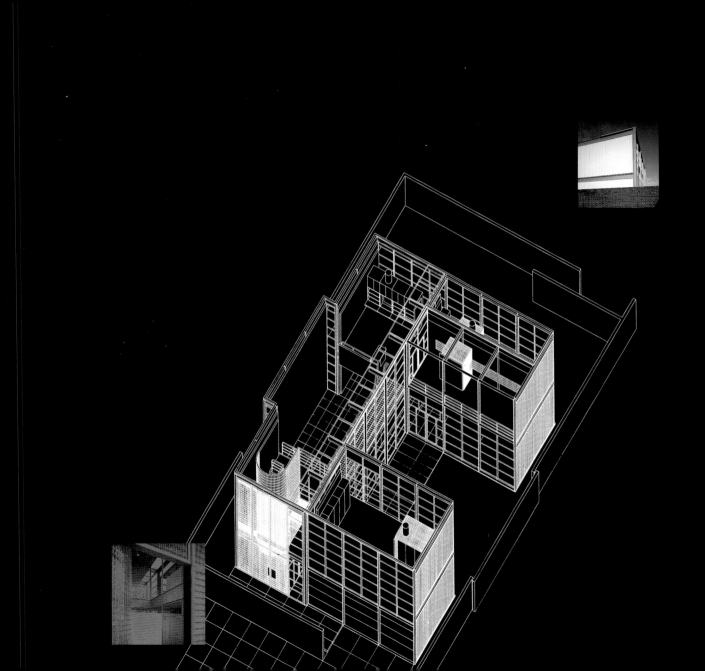

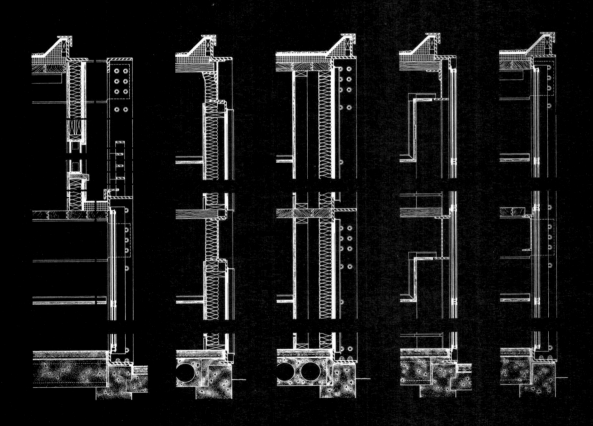

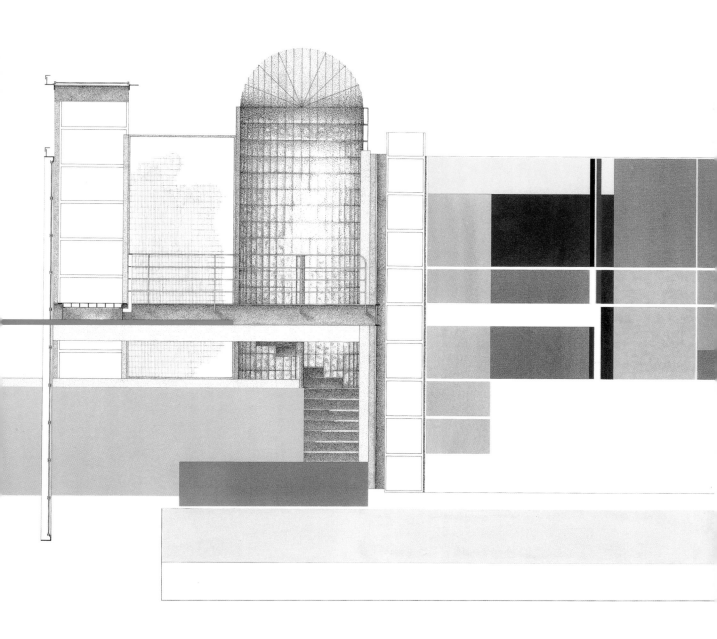

The mural of the Steel and Glass House

– what was and what wasn't –

became the basis for the initial studies of the Thonet Showroom. In the residence, the **forces**
of the architectural elements are tightly contained rectangles. In the Thonet Showroom, the **forces**
of the rectangles are released, literally projected by painted diagrams of their implied **forces**
onto the walls, floors, and ceilings.

Thonet Industries is a prominent, Pennsylvania-based furniture manufacturer. The company's
wish to create an innovative environment in which to display their furniture elicited a study
of light, color, and texture. The space became a series of projections and layered
transparencies in which rectangles had been stretched, leaving traces of their architectural
history. The showroom is a composite of two designs: the first is an analytical diagram of the
architectural elements of the preexisting space; the second is the interventions of the new
scheme and their expanded energies – an attempt to bring the first analysis into equilibrium.

The result of superimposing both plans establishes a new set of spatial associations.

The showroom is punctuated with perforated metal screens of different densities, acrylic lens
panels, and linear arrangements of floor-to-ceiling fluorescent lights of different colors.
Their forms are suggestive of transparent planes that activate and structure the space of the
showroom. These new forms are reinforced and further integrated with the existing elements
through a carefully considered palette of paint colors that create transparent veils. The effect is
an illusionary perception of a space that has no physical boundaries. Thonet's classic Bentwood
Chair changes color as it passes through the light and space, becoming a focus so that viewers
might extend their thoughts and
imagine themselves projected
through this delineated sequence.

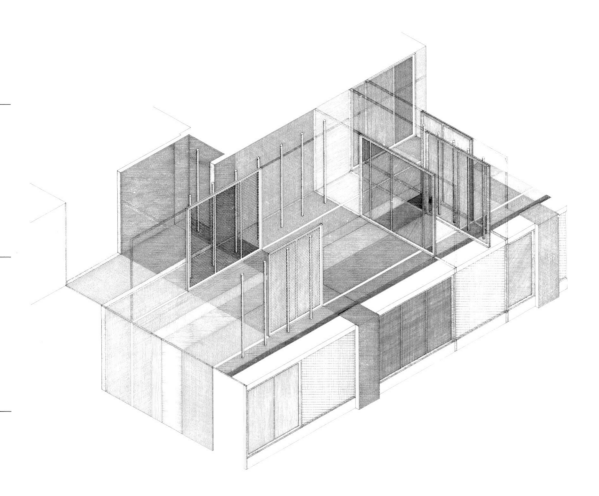

This apartment is on the north side of Chicago and overlooks Lincoln Park and Lake Michigan. **The client was no longer interested in living with paintings hanging on the walls but wanted to be surrounded by an integral work of art: to live within a painting.** The space was originally a three-bedroom apartment in a gridded Mies high-rise with a surreal view of the lake and park. The window wall, between columns and from floor to ceiling, is a single expanse of glass. We eliminated all walls, except those enclosing the kitchen and bathrooms. A fifty-five-foot stainless-steel platform extends the length of the window wall. At three points this glistening mass projects out into the space to accept velvet mattresses and a banquette, and at two points it pulls back to ease movement between the centralized living space and the sleeping areas at either end of the apartment. The central column in the living space causes distortions and reverberations that undulate throughout the composition. At the perimeter, the rectilinear qualities are brought back into resolution. The forces that caused the overlapping and stretched rectangles of the Thonet Showroom have in the Painted Apartment become warped and torn.

Curving glass-block walls are illuminated from within and provide lighting. Functional separations are created by sliding panels and wardrobes, which are finished with highly polished metallic automobile paints. The central area is manipulated by perforated-metal screens of different densities, which combine to form a multitude of patterns that activate the space and give it a kinetic energy. The oscillation of these screens recalls Moholy-Nagy's 1930 sculpture "Light-Space Modulator." The fluctuations of the space are caused by graduated dot openings in the screens, which, depending on the light of day, are either transparent, translucent, or reflective. Floors, ceilings, and perimeter walls shimmer with glossy paint in a range of seven grays and three accent colors (which dissolve into stenciled dots that make continuous the path of the screens), vertically extending the horizontal layers of the space. This graceful ebb and flow of the re-created Lake Michigan shoreline is echoed in the veils between the living and dining areas. The forms of the furniture were designed in specific response to the space and are an integral part of the final **composition**.

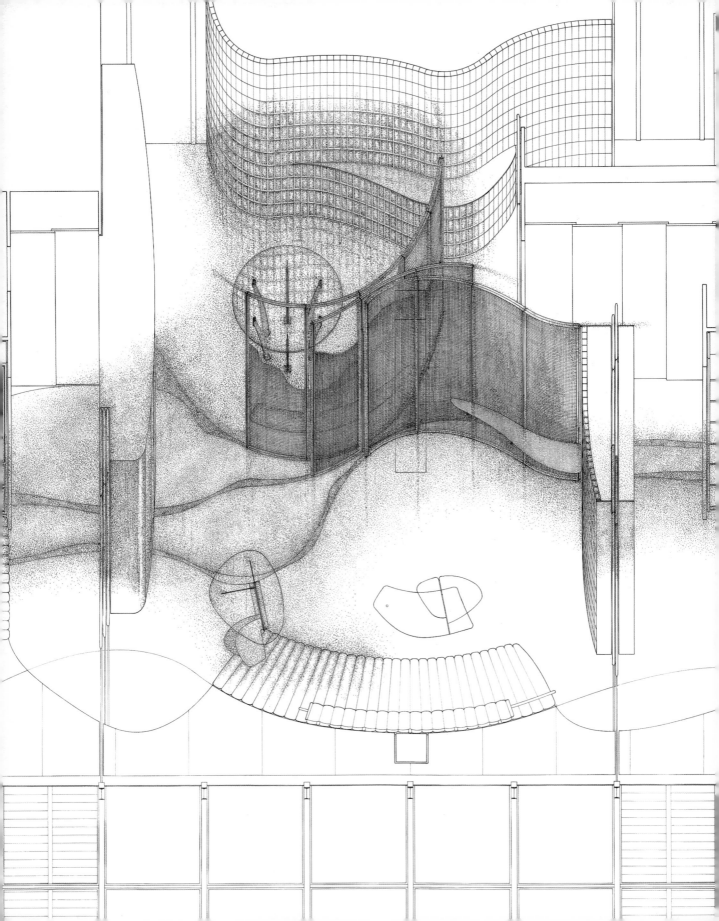

This project is for a family with seven children who had purchased a Victorian townhouse in an architectural preservation district on the Near North Side of Chicago. Due to this location, alterations were not permitted to the street facade; however, there were no restrictions in the rear. We envisioned the transition from the unchanged period facade through carefully renovated interiors to a baroque architectural garden as a conscious effort to expand the space through time, from the formal receiving rooms to the informal living spaces and terraced deck of the extensions of the house.

The extension and its living areas are constructed of faceted surfaces of pinned multicolored mirrored glass, aluminum panels, and perforated metal screens, which are used to veil and channel views. Glass-block floors and ceilings allow maximum light in the dense urban setting. Horizontal and vertical planes are tapered, emphasizing their edges, diminishing their mass, and helping to capture the space. Canopies give a sense of privacy and enclosure from the surrounding high-rises. Many of the aluminum components take their cues from the wings of an airplane, as they resist the pressure beneath them and project themselves outward to control the space. The rectangular forms of the Steel and Glass House have here been torn apart, faceted, bent, tapered, and reflected infinitely into themselves, thus acquiring new freedoms. In a heroic gesture, the rectilinear structure punctures the perimeter walls to become dominant. These theoretical freedoms were the basis for the design of our next several projects, in which they would be overlapped, inverted, and vertically extended.

In the original portion of the house, a complete spectrum of colors was used to refinish the original moldings and trim, which eliminated the Victorian sensation of weight and closure; instead, the moldings appear to emanate light.

The furniture and cabinetry clearly respond to the plaster cove moldings in each room. These moldings disappear as one moves through the space until they dissolve, becoming knife edges at the rear of the residence. This movement marks the passage through time; at each transition the space is completely synchronized.

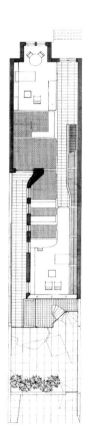 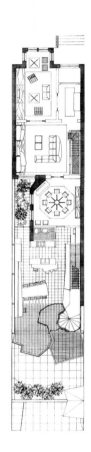 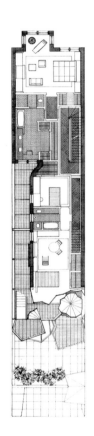 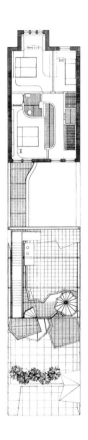

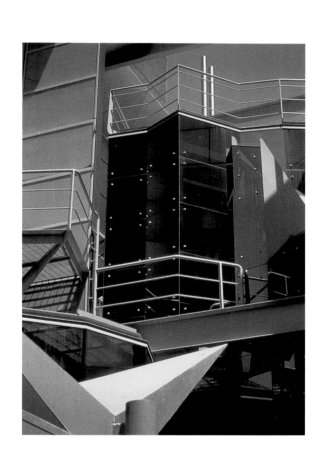

This 6,500-square-foot duplex apartment is for a couple who wanted to live with their heads in the clouds and their hands in the earth; they now refer to their home as their "space-age capsule." We resisted seduction by the spectacular panoramic views outside the two-story window wall that surrounds the residence on three sides by orienting the duplex inward to develop an **i n t e r i o r   l a n d s c a p e .** The interior space is separated from the perimeter by a sequence of stone terraces that smooth the transition to the window wall. The living spaces are arranged around a central atrium enclosed by two levels of curved glass boundaries that play concave against convex from floor to floor. These glass walls appear to be suspended within the building envelope, boomeranging and colliding to create an illusion of perpetual motion. All forms are streamlined and their surfaces are either transparent or reflective, radiating a tightly keyed palette of silvers and golds; various granites cover floors, stairs, platforms, and counters; and muted reflective paints coat the cabinetry. This subtle palette resulted from our desire to allow each element its appropriate density and each movement its appropriate speed within the c   o   m   p   o   s   i   t   i   o   n   .

On the second floor are sleeping areas and a study that are connected by a textured plate-glass bridge. No space on the second floor touches the perimeter, reinforcing a sense of floating planes. A translucent glass ceiling overlaps various elements and begins to integrate these spaces, while dispersing light to the architectural garden below. A cantilevered glass stair projects into the atrium and rises above a reflecting pool lined in black granite that mirrors the plan of the glass bridge. This residual form of the convex and concave movements of the glass atrium enclosure causes visual oscillations that are yet another extension of the kinetic abstractions that are a continuing preoccupation in our **w   o   r   k   .** The composition is pulled vertically and develops strong literal and implied transparencies. Qualities that had previously occurred only in plan and elevation are now developed in section. Mirrored and transparent glass forms allow for extension or refraction of the space. These desired illusions are amplified by detailing minimal connections between the glass planes. The fluid qualities of this space, like that of the Painted Apartment, appear to expand and contract gently while always acknowledging the orthogonal geometries of the high-rise building. The functions of the high-rise controlled and limited movement within the original space. It was the attempt to liberate these restrictions that put the initial pushing and pulling in motion, resulting in forces that were not applied, but rather found. We believe that while working on a project, certain forces begin to emerge and to take precedence, telling the architect what to do.

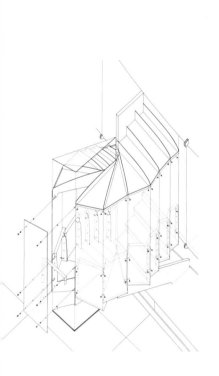

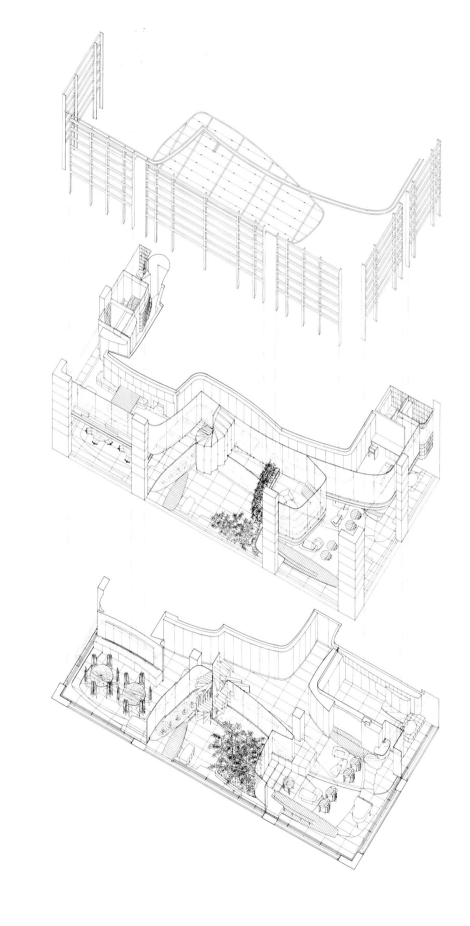

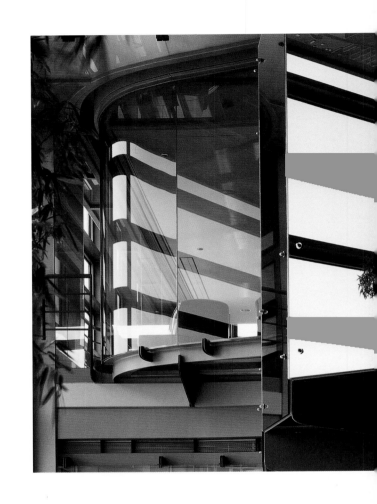

The plan expresses the elaborate interdependencies developed among the functional forms. The controlling forces and their fragments are evident upon arrival. These elements create a stratification that is evidenced in the plan, which is composed of fifteen horizontal sections. The cubist nature of the space is experienced in the juxtaposition of the masses and planes; their interaction molds the furniture and creates sculpted surfaces that carefully guide the participant through the apartment while simultaneously responding to the innumerable detailed functional requirements of the clients. Their wish was not to have a home in the sky; rather, they wanted an urban apartment, where efficiency was maximized and maintenance minimized. Just as the design of an airplane fuselage is dictated by aerodynamics and internal requirements, so the molded surfaces of this apartment were developed. The highly defined program accounts not only for the precise living environment, but also for the very shape and form. Greatest use was made of storage space, tailoring the cabinetwork to specific functions. All items may be easily stored away, maintaining day-to-day the streamlined forms that allow for ease of movement while accentuating the speed of their edges. No embellishments were required in this space, where the slightest move or change in light establishes new compositions of form and color. The stratification of the space that occurred in Untitled No. 1 was elaborated upon and amplified in this project, as the curves of the different horizontal layers were compressed and different fluid shapes were developed at various elevations between floor and ceiling. The density of the sculpted forms that define the entry is transformed through the gallery to generate a more expansive living environment at the perimeter. Here, only furniture elements and faceted surfaces of glass separate functions. The curves of the apartment suggest sculptural origins, resembling Calder mobiles; slowing down, they give way to the rectilinear edges of the building. An inner plane was applied to the perimeter of the apartment, diminishing the mass of the columns and creating continuous viewing frames that read as a series of paperlike cutouts. We maintained a quiet control: curves appear in profusion, but never without a reason, and their expression is always taut and appropriate. A palette of more than fifty colors was created in order to articulate the masses, yet the range is severely limited to give a cohesive quality to the space. Every intersection is resolved; one element discreetly folds or pulls back to allow another to pass; and dominant forces are always maintained, allowing this Schwitters-like environment to be analyzed and resolved.

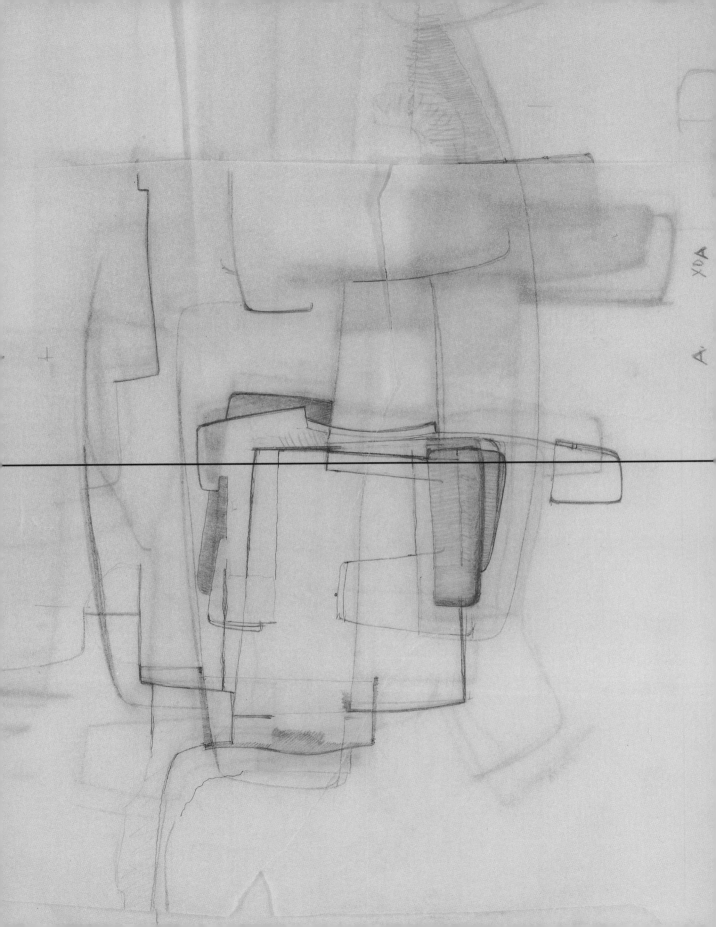

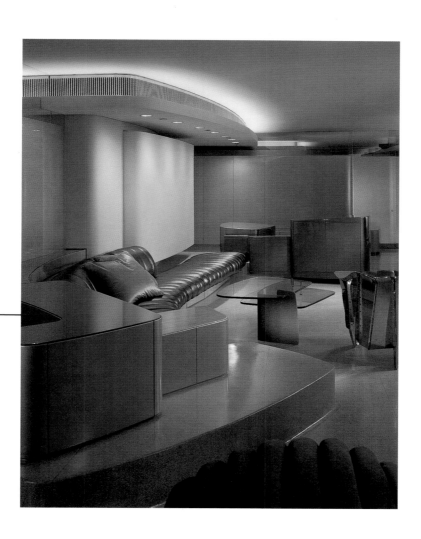

The evolution of our architecture required not only that the built-in furniture be designed, but also that the freestanding furniture be an extension of the aesthetics of the spaces. Paradoxically, each organically inspired piece appears to be a celebration of industrial design, while in reality they are all meticulously handmade. OLYMPIAN I The back of this dining chair evokes the discreetly folded wings of an insect. The anodized aluminum perforated screens of the chair rise high above the table to encompass the space. These screens develop an intimacy while the perforations allow for veiled views of the dining area and the spaces beyond. RK CHAISE The spine, a series of vertebrae with extended ribs, is the inspiration for this chaise, which is structured by a continuous line of cut and bent stainless-steel plates. The cushions are individual modules of upholstery connected at each rib. OLYMPIAN II The least organic of our furniture, this dining chair has been reduced to its minimal functional form. It is defined by the restrained curves that free its internal energies. Stainless-steel plates have been bent and openings milled out only as required to develop pulls and handles. THE CHICAGO CHAIR The fluid qualities of the stainless steel and the precision of the machined metal plates contrast with the sensual forms of the plush velvet upholstery. The Chicago Chair's reflections dissolve into themselves, dematerializing, as the stainless-steel arms unfold seductively to invite one **to rest upon the yielding fabric.**

The site is the piano nobile of an 1891 Stanford White mansion on Chicago's Gold Coast. The client fully appreciated the grandeur and craftsmanship of the great old rooms but did not want to re-create the late Victorian lifestyle and genteel and cluttered spaces of the original owners. Instead, the client wanted a spartan interior within which one could both easily move and be comfortable. **We focused first on restoring the spirit and elegance of White's nineteenth-century classicism. The piano nobile had originally been reception rooms, which the developers had partially broken down to provide the accommodations required for an apartment. As a result, scale, proportion, and materials had been disrupted. We wanted to return the space to its original grandeur, restoring the detail of the public rooms with meticulous attention, while carrying the same decorum into the private quarters. Certain liberties were taken in attempting to recapture the spirit of the era, such as extending moldings to create light coves that amplify the crown moldings and pulling fireplace hearths across rooms to establish appropriate scale.** Having accomplished this, we introduced a different vision, one integrating historic elegance with the modern vocabulary of the late twentieth century. The sleek forms of grandly scaled furniture and cabinetwork finished in contemporary materials befitting the richness of the house were inserted into the harmonious and restrained container. The dialogue between the container and the contained amplifies the qualities of both, and though they appear at first to be as far apart as the waltz is from the tango, their underpinnings are of the same sensitivities and therefore a real understanding is established. The curves we used throughout White's sequence of rectangles give them a dynamic, in much the same way Le Corbusier countered the rigid grid of the Villa Savoye with the curves of the entrance and terrace.

The entry walls, finished in high-gloss gold lacquer, curve to rotate the initial axis and gracefully reinforce the passage into the living room and parlor. The reflection of the elliptical curve of the walls is incised into the carpet, as are the lines of other architectural forces generated by this rotation of the axis. The carpet incorporates the palette of colors found throughout the apartment. The living room furniture, of granite, marble, and polished millwork, is of the deepest saturated colors, balancing the visual weight of the restored English brown oak walls. The curves of the furniture define the edge of the living space and cause one to pause before proceeding to the dining area. Here, the impressive oak paneling recedes to give way to a free-form beveled glass table with a base of patinated and polished bronze that extends to provide support for the burgundy marble serving surface. A warped plane of gold is suspended above the table and compresses the space to the edges. The perimeter is lined with bronze-framed, backlit glass doors that replace Stanford White's missing library doors and create walls of light with infinite reflections. This vision is one where the past and the present have been woven inseparably together. On the other side of the entrance is a curving hall, a time warp of polished ebony and gold surfaces to the futuristic stage set of the sleeping area. This insulated bedroom, freed from historic influences, is a composition of black granite slab floors, sculpted high-gloss cabinets, and faceted backlit panels of translucent glass that wrap the room on two edges.

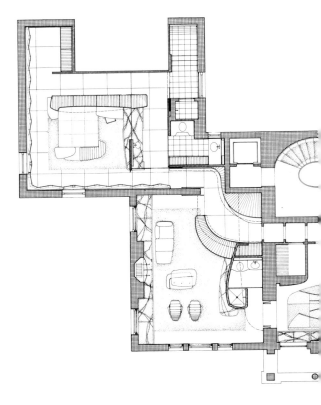

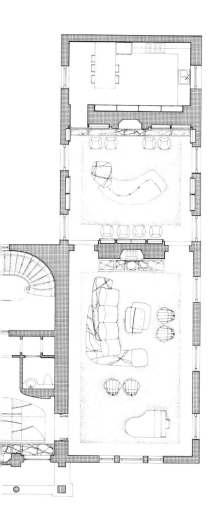

A forty-two-acre oak forest frames the three structures we developed as the campus headquarters of Hewitt Associates, an international benefits consulting firm. The trees were considered sacred; their position determined the location of buildings and parking.

First seen through the densely wooded site, the headquarters appears as hovering volumes. The subtleties of the curtain wall are obscured by the natural rhythm of the woods. Seen at a closer range, the differentiating mullions create major and minor systems of overlapping rectangles. Vertically, the modulation is broken down as the second floor is pushed eight inches in front of the rest of the facade; it appears higher than the other stories since it incorporates the bottom spandrel of the third floor. At the entrance, the facade is eroded, allowing the cedar siding to remain in plane while the glass is pushed back, clarifying the parts and defining the initial edges of the modulations.

The primary functions, efficiently tailored to Hewitt's needs, became the foundation of the building's design. All professional personnel receive ten-by-twelve-and-one-half-foot offices; typically, rows of these offices alternate with corridors that widen to accommodate secretaries and shared equipment. Hewitt requested that there be no expression of hierarchy in the plan of the offices and that all corners be assigned to conference or joint work rooms. This regularity created complete flexibility, allowing for changes in personnel without requiring alterations. Inside, each private office was provided with simple built-in wall-to-wall counters to accommodate equipment and reams of spreadsheets. So that the offices could take full advantage of the exterior, the three narrow wings of the building are extended into the forest. The regularity of the office areas required that the corridors be kept short and take strong orientation cues from the central core and the four-story atrium. The atrium is a composition of floating planes that are painted in bleached-out natural colors and bathed in light from perimeter skylights at the entry. One of the exterior curtain walls slides into the atrium and leaves its impression etched into the wall before receding. This space, the town center of the building, is enhanced by its scale, centralized circulation system, and the reflections of natural light.

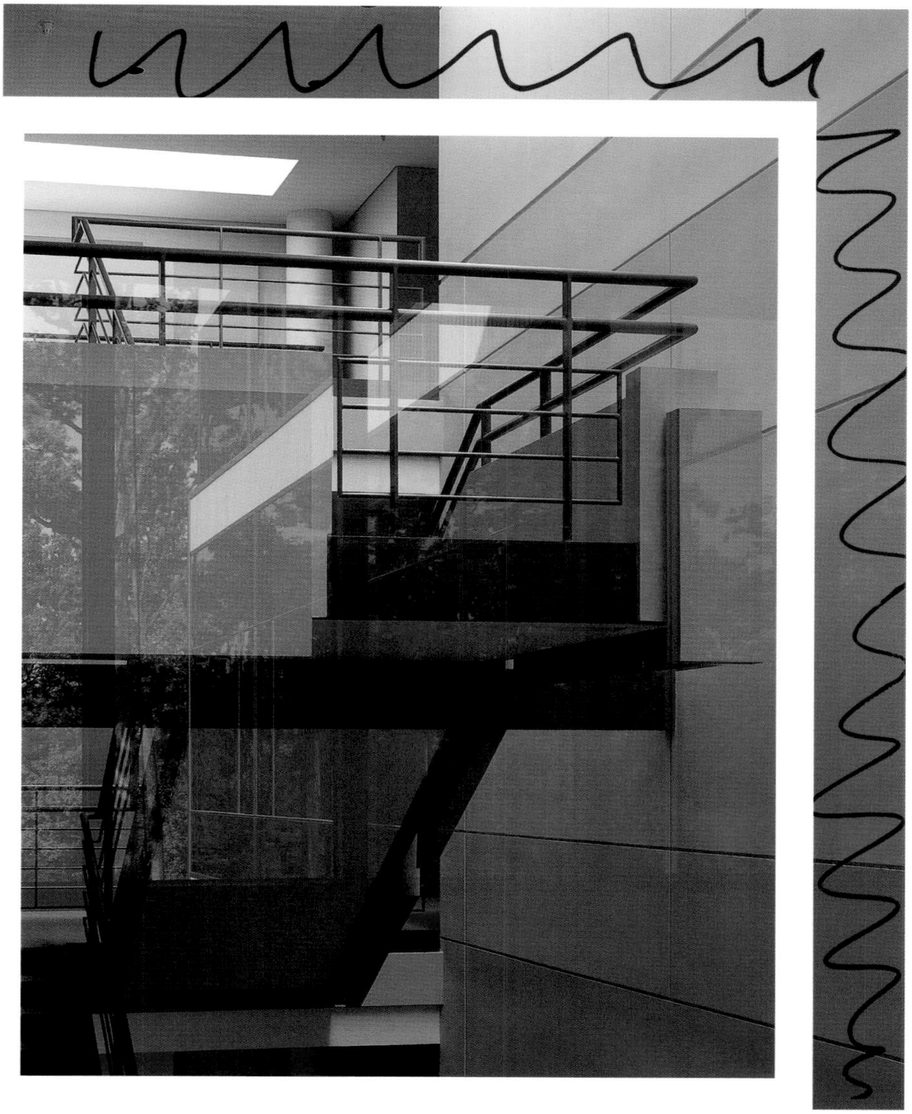

Rockledge is a fifteen-acre estate that overlooks the Long Island Sound; its turn-of-the-century manor house is listed in the National Register of Historic Places. The thirty-six-thousand-square-foot house had been carefully restored and the great rooms were converted into a major conference center. The objectives of the project were to provide office space for two hundred employees and also to reinforce the qualities of the estate. During the design evolution of the new building, rigid mass and building systems were fractured into two primary rectangular fragments, reducing the scale of the structure to the site. These two elements were then arranged around a two-story atrium developed as a composition of overlapping planes in plan and their vertical extension in section. It is here that the reverberations of the initial break continue to be felt and the more expressive elements of the building are exposed.

Around the two skewed office fragments is a curtain-wall system of contemporary components; it has an arrangement of mullions that complements the proportions of the mansion windows. The arrangement was derived from the projection of the interior systems onto the adjacent facades. Cross corridors shift the office cores by half a module from the perimeter system. This shift initiates major and minor modulations in the elevation and establishes a system of overlapping planes of glass and granite in subdued colors. Each elevation is symmetrical, acknowledging the formal qualities of the mansion's front. On another scale, the building is keyed into the site by a plinth that extends the aesthetics of the building into the landscape. The east side of the plinth is also one edge of the building; here the curtain wall extends past this edge to read as a suspended plane.

The facade pattern erodes as it approaches the fractured and transparent employee entrance. This allows the larger moves of the atrium to sustain their own integrity, while still allowing integration with the overall facades. New juxtapositions of forms and new freedoms of space result from the disruption to the building's orthogonal grid. With this fracturing, the functional elements become exposed and are therefore more expressive. The precise forms and their composition evolved through a repetitive process of superimposing and distilling the conflicting energies in the space. Ceiling heights, clerestories, and the edges of bridges are the result of this process in section. These forms are reintegrated into the final solution so that nothing appears out of place. The openness and dynamics of the atrium respond to the modulation of the adjacent facades. Its forms, while signifying entry and expressing the movement of the circulation system, appear to be in suspended animation.

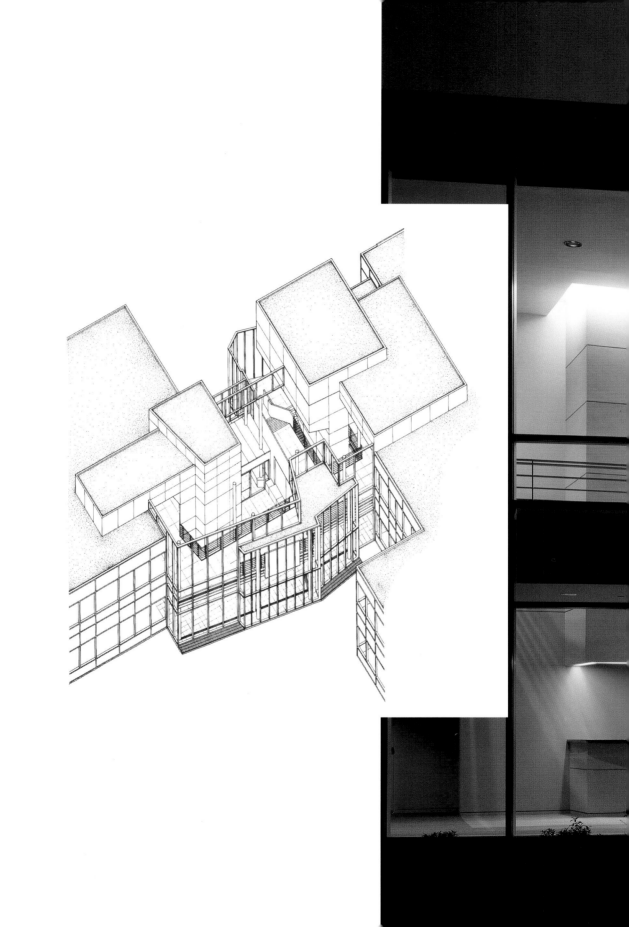

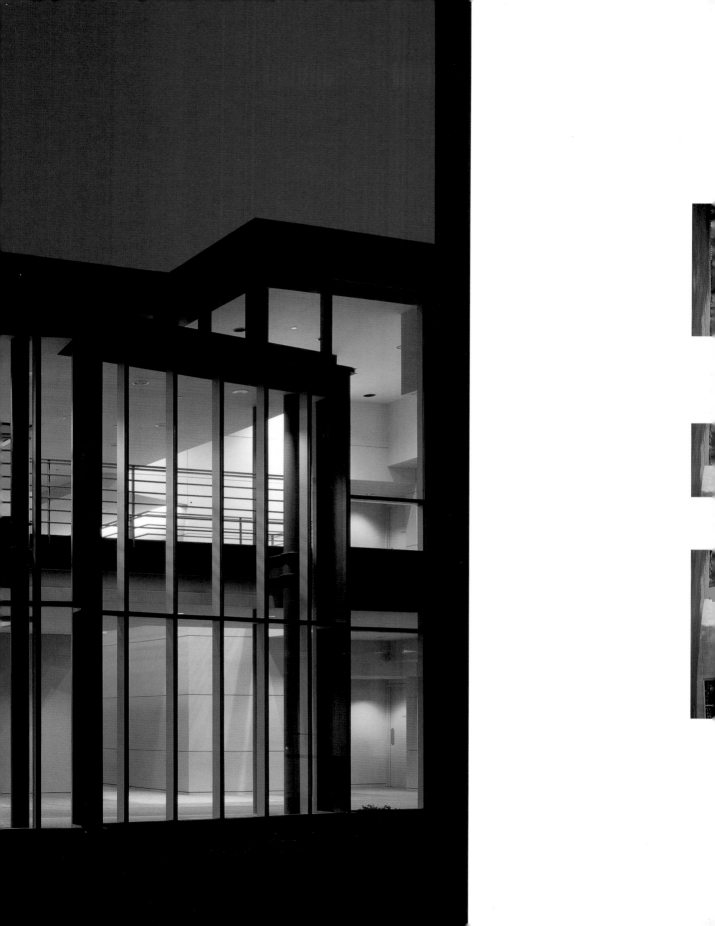

This 3,400-square-foot duplex for a young family of four is on the top floors of a Mies van der Rohe steel-and-glass apartment tower with magnificent views of the lake and city. Here the rotations, warpings, fracturing, and inversion of the rectangle in our work have been brought to rest as if a plateau had been achieved. ■■■■ The earlier Steel and Glass House may be compared to Mondrian's classic and calm compositions of red, yellow, and blue. In this project the space is once again composed of rectangles that rest at right angles to each other but are not serene and perfectly resolved; they are more like the pulsating, energetic rectangles of Mondrian's late painting "Broadway Boogie-Woogie." This project has dynamics that did not, and could not, exist in the previous work. Our resolution of the space appears as a synthesis of the freedoms found in previous searches. The tight floor plate and gridded construction insisted that the fundamental architectural strengths of the rectangle would reappear. ■■■■■■■■■

Initially, **we cut a slot into the floor**. Acting like a magnet, it internalizes and inhibits the flow of space. The soffits, while **reinforcing the vertical reading of the two-story space**, simultaneously compress and extend it to the exterior of the building and incorporate it within the gridded urban fabric of the cityscape. The informal living spaces of the kitchen, dining, study, and children's bedrooms are located on the lower level and are linked by a stainless-steel stair through the slot to the formal living area, office, and master bedroom of the upper level. The clients wanted a minimally furnished and dynamic space constructed of durable materials; the major materials — glass-chip terrazzo, plates of stainless steel, and cabinets wrapped in colored stainless steel — were used for their visual strength and ease of maintenance as well. ■■■■■■■■■■

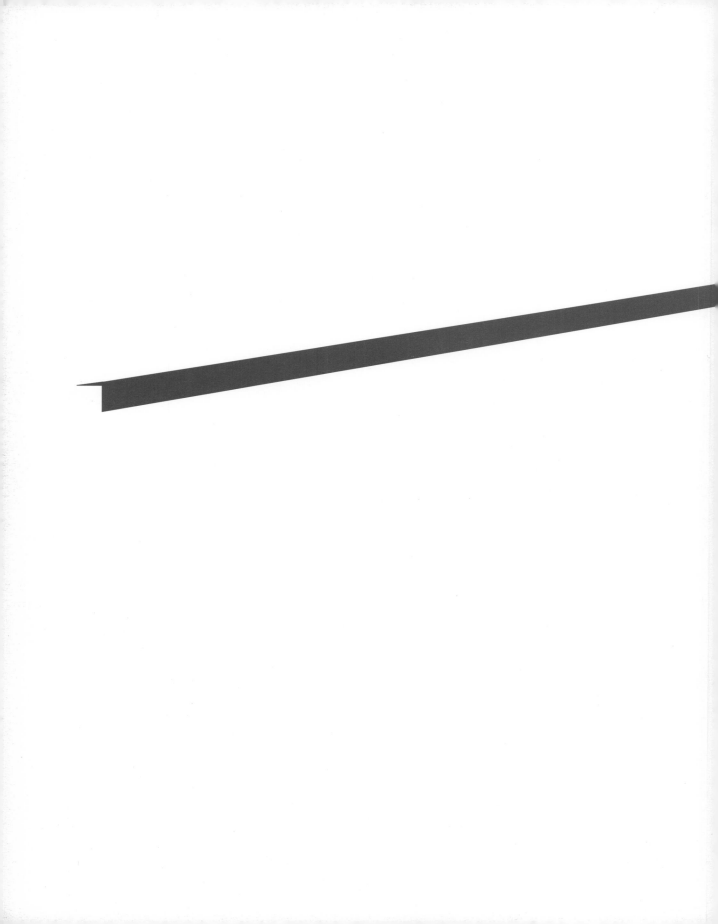

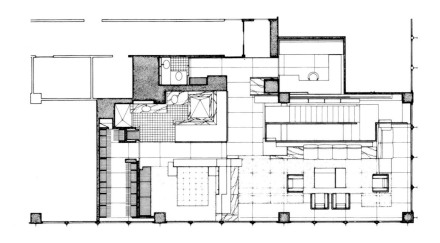

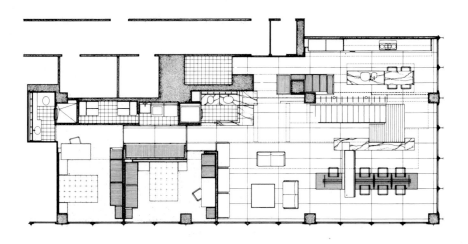

This ground-level bank is on Wilshire Boulevard and
serves as a retail trust facility that also fulfills the office requirements for the trust officers
and investors. The retail banking area was to recall the spatial qualities of earlier grand banking halls.
Here, we established a rectangle in plan, while the section is warped. This warp takes advantage of the
twenty-foot-high space and responds to the program, which required all areas of the bank to exploit the
limited natural light that filters in from only one elevation. After the acoustics and the reflections of light
were studied, a gently arched wing of curly maple veneers was designed and stretched the length of the
space, allowing light to be evenly dispersed and sounds to be softened. A core of conference rooms was
developed and placed to separate the public banking area from the offices. The arc of the conference core
and vault responds to the pressures of the suspended wing. These moves initiate the modulations of the
space and finally establish their synchroneity. All transactions take place with sit-down tellers, reinforcing
a relaxed image of personalized service. A natural palette of wood veneers and Greek white
and dark green marbles was selected to express the traditional heritage and strength of this

hundred-year-old Midwestern institution that now serves the dynamic environment of Los Angeles.

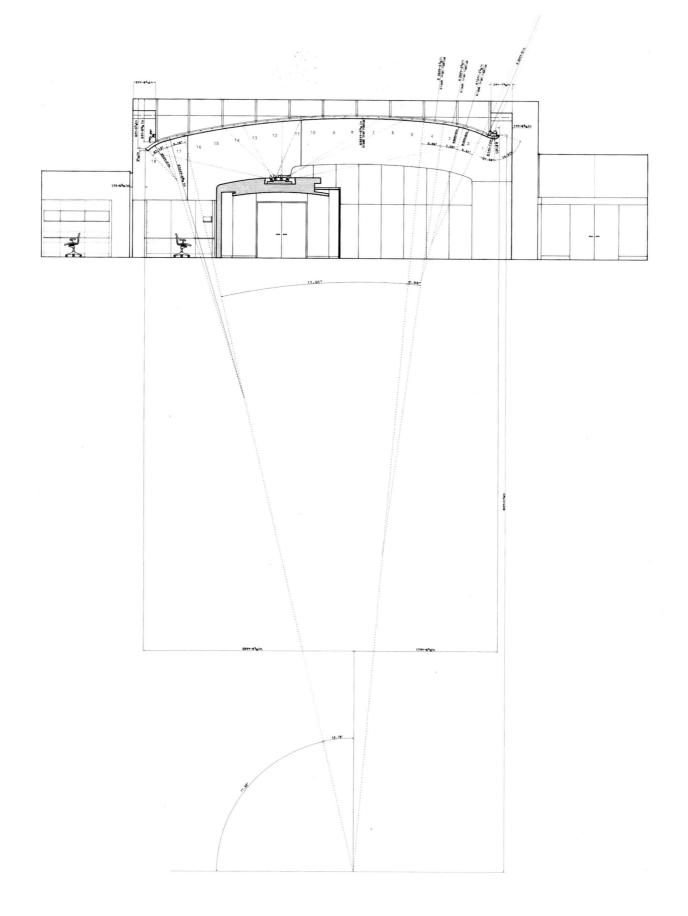

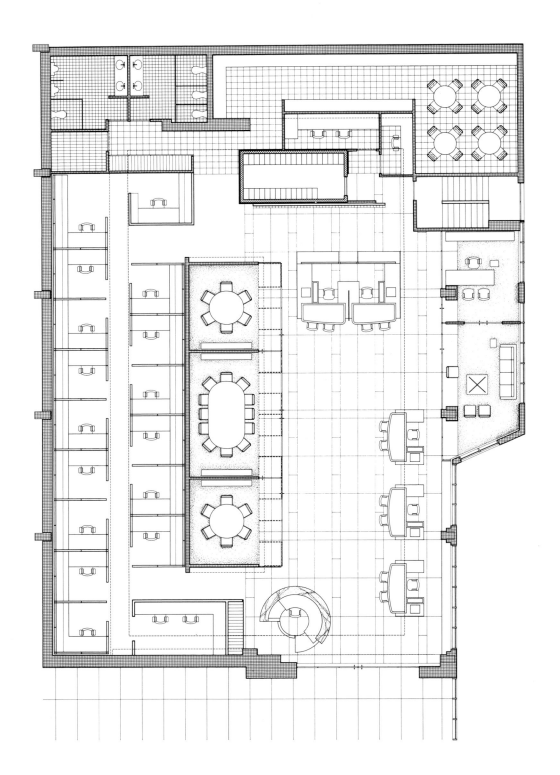

This house is adjacent to a picturesque, residential, planned unit development. The owners, a couple with two young children, were dissatisfied with the constraints imposed by the typical city lot and initiated the search for this site, where they wanted a residence with continuous living spaces that would be appreciated as a whole. The house is positioned on the one-hundred-by-eighty-foot site with its narrow elevation parallel to the street; this intentionally breaks the rhythm of the adjacent facades and visually achieves an independence for the house while allowing vistas of the Georgian-style community.

We perceived the house as the intersection of two opaque and two transparent rectangles. The major masonry rectangle is intersected from the street elevation by a block of limestone, which is carved out to allow for three garages. Its surfaces extend to the far edges of two steel canopies that slide out from dense facades to indicate entry: one has translucent glass doors for service; the other, more formal, a clear glass vestibule that extends out to signify the public entrance. This vestibule is bisected by a planar extension of the limestone block. Its low height causes one to pause and assess the weights and balances of the composition of the two-story centralized space. This living space was developed by eroding the brick volume. Two L-shaped masonry fragments remained and appeared to stand in isolation at either end of this elevation until the insertion of a glass rectangle. Two T shapes built up of elongated glass rectangles stretch, trying to complete the enclosure of the garden facade. Instead, the living space interrupts and projects in front of the existing windows a new two-story glass wall of freer geometries that express its independence. The original elongated gridded glass wall slides into the interior of this new volume, completing, on one side of the second floor, the master bedroom and, on the other side, the library. The fourth rectangle, a glass crystal, is inserted into this composition and appears as a slot on the street elevation; it crosses the roof as a continuous skylight, bathing the public areas of the house with diffused natural light.

As geometries were completed, freedoms respected, and conflicts identified, breaks developed in the original rectangle. Further clarification required shifts in section. A greater resolution was accomplished in the two-story living space, where the collision of the primary rectangles was resolved. Edges were located off the grid, establishing a new module the thickness of the red line. Unlike the proposed mural for the Steel and Glass House, here the mural is not painted on one plane. First, sectional moves begin to incorporate the space into the wall. Then the architectural elements are integrated into the composition of the mural, drawing imperceptible boundaries between what is and what isn't. This ambiguity insists that one's spatial perceptions be continuously adjusted.

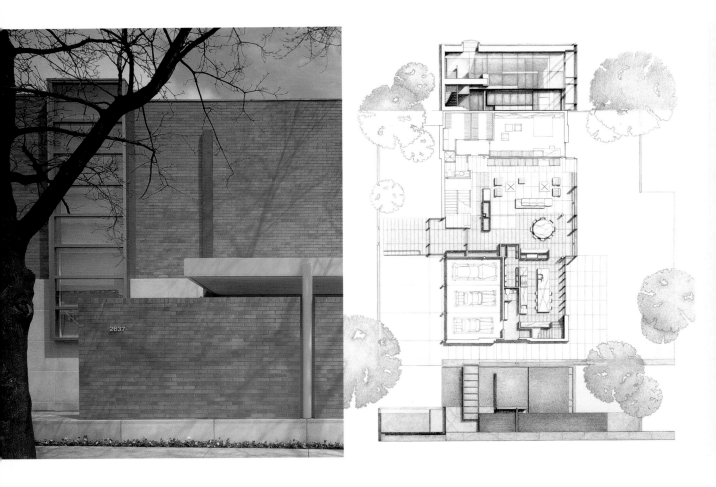

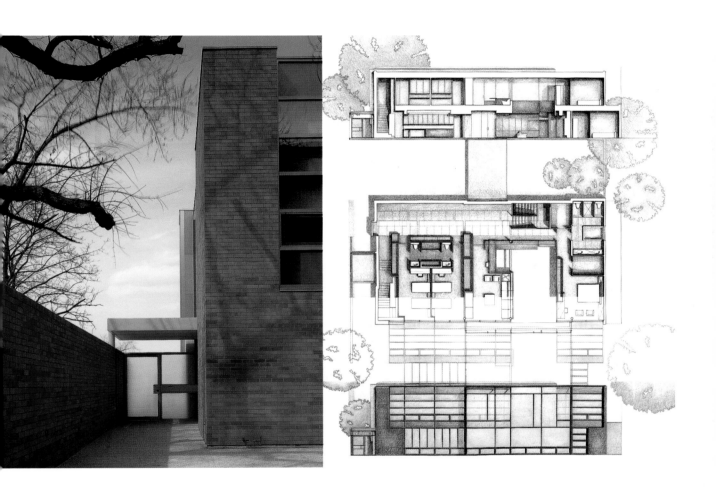

This unbuilt residence for a single family was to be located on the edge of Lincoln Park with Lake Michigan in the not-too-distant backgroun. The site imposed very specific restrictions: on one side is a large mansion of historic significance; on the other side and at the rear, modest nineteenth-centu row houses provide the boundarie.

Garden walls, lot-line bearing walls, and a screen wall comprise the concrete envelope. These walls provide the edges of a momentary interruption to th block and also respond contextually to the limestone and terra-cotta buildings of the neighborhood, while protecting the glass perimeter of the living spac.

The interior space is articulated by forms, surfaces, and voids that respond freely to the functional requirements, including the display of a major collectio of paintings and sculptures. The living spaces are raised above the ground to provide the best views of the park and lake. The ground floor contains an entran hall and vestibule. A children's playroom adjoins the partially covered courtyard. Elevated platforms for sculpture and a front stair ascend to the living spa on the floor above. The main stair gives access to all levels and separates the living spaces from the servants' quarters, garage, storage, and service entranc which are accessible from a side street. On the main floor, the reception hall is screened from the multistory living room by platforms, openings to the floor belo and a twenty-foot mural. The dining area is a fluctuating four-story space, manipulated by a series of cutouts in the floor and ceilings. Sliding panels can separa these public areas from the family-oriented spaces of the kitchen and more informal parts of the house. In the courtyard, a bridge and a sculpture platform a suspended, connecting the formal and informal living spaces physically as well as visually. On the second floor, the master bedroom has remarkable views the park and lake; it is an element wedged into the two-story living space and linked to the stair by a balcony that traverses the dining area below. A library a study are located behind the screen of the main staircase. Children's rooms and baths are on the third level, with a sundeck and entertainment facilities at t front overlooking the park. The concrete screen walls rise above this floor in order to give a sense of enclosure to the exterior spac.

The rigid envelope of concrete is manipulated to create security, both psychological and physical, and to contrast with the more delicate objects of facete mirrored glass of varying colors and densities. It is as if a rectangular block of stone had been carved away, leaving its frame to protect the precious crystals th had been exposed. The courtyard walls are punctured, warped, and tapered to emphasize the edges, diminish their mass, and encompass the space, allowi the inhabitants distinct and articulated views of the pa.

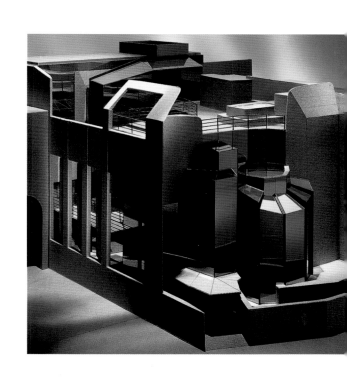

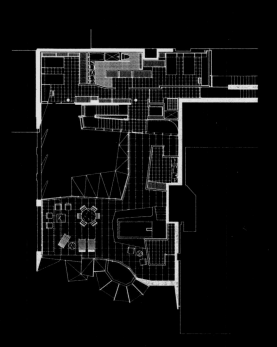

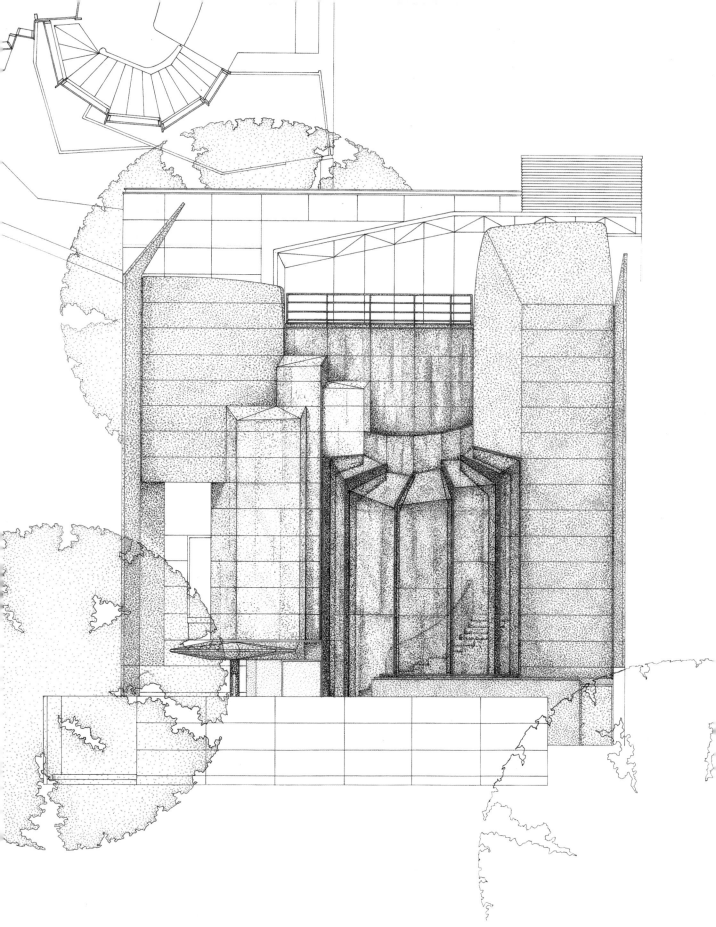

This free public library was the gift of the American people to the people of Berlin after World War II. The library expansion was an invited competition of fourteen American architects. The program required that the square footage be more than doubled; the major restraint was that the original tower could not be touched. The solution could have easily fractured into parts as a result of these demands. Instead, to integrate the tower into the composition completely, we treated it as if it were one of Rauschenberg's found objects, discovered and then collaged between the new components of the program.

We planned the Blucherplatz, in front of the library, as a large paved plaza; it provides space for various activities, such as street theater, festivals, and markets. A recessed amphitheater expands the library's cultural offerings to the outdoors. A sequence of gridded paving, green areas, orchards, and pools of water extends the aesthetics and releases the architecture from within the new library. This extended frame provides a green space and a relaxed environment adjacent to the library.

This major plaza creates a proper foreground for the library, which we developed to the east. The facade of the original building tower is retained as the prominent terminus of the Friedrichstrasse. The new building is lifted from the ground on concrete columns to maintain an exterior path through the new architectural elements to the historic park at the rear. This establishes in plan an interaction between the building and the Blucherplatz. The new entrance provides direct access to the ground-floor public spaces, such as the auditorium, exhibition space, browsing room, and main library circulation desk. The children's library is located in the remodeled space of the old reading rooms. Other subject areas have been arranged on four higher stories. Each floor is connected via a glass-enclosed link to the original library tower, allowing staff access to each level of the existing library. This connection then overlaps the tower and opens into a winter garden for public use, while preserving the identity of the original structure. A visual integration of the complex is achieved by collaging the old structure between, on one side, the new sculpted forms of the auditorium and the punctured planes of the entry that reinforce the foreground and, on the other, the new highly articulated block of varying densities that establishes the background.

The circulation zone, a transparent shaft of light that severs the floor plates, is on axis with a late-nineteenth-century church to the east and is terminated by a glass-enclosed ramp that connects each level. The continuation of the circulation system, a spiral stair with a constantly moving center that is reminiscent of the sculptures of Frank Stella, insists on being the vertical focus of this zone. Glass-floored bridges cross the circulation zone, while a fractured clerestory skylight amplifies the movements at the roof. All glass in this zone is the same structural glazing, while the remaining curtain wall has greater articulation and is further defined by different colored glass running vertically, which reflects the library stack modules.

The aluminum-framed wings of perforated metal screen the north view, visually quieting the library. The wings also establish an important architectural device that scoops the space of the plaza into the library. The concrete structural grid is shifted in response to the site. This move is expressed by pulling the window wall forward, allowing the rational and inevitable rectilinear structure to be completely exposed on the south facade.

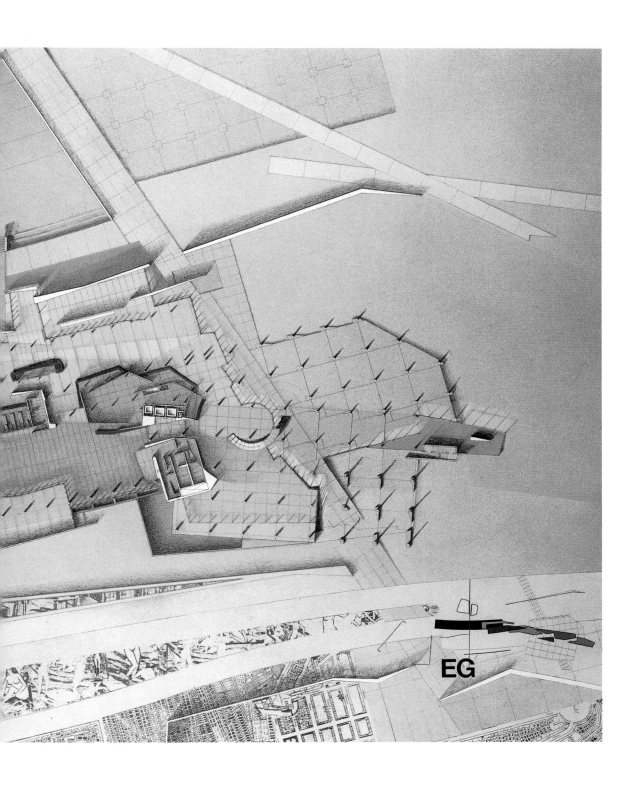

EG

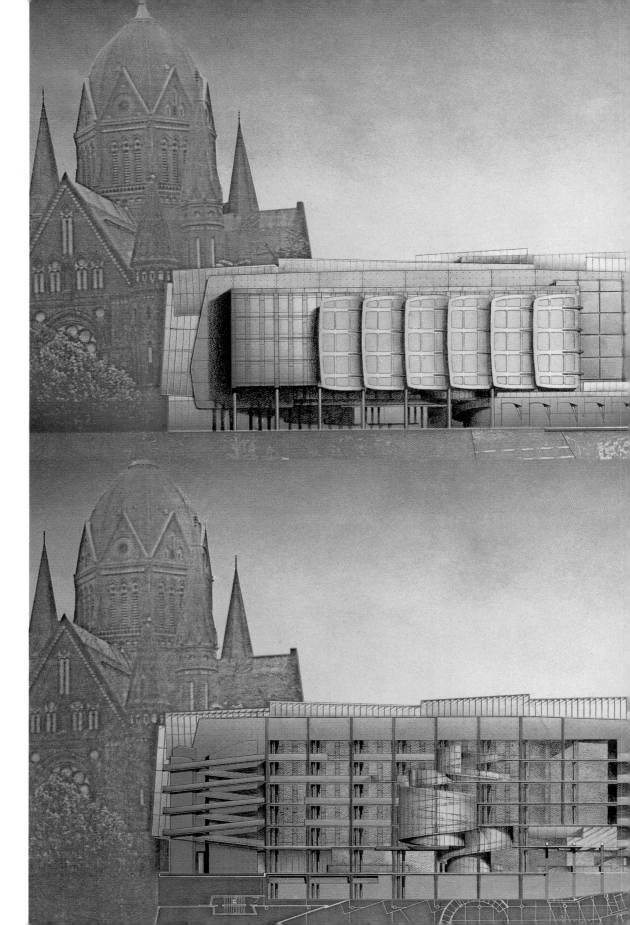

For decades, the Arts Club of Chicago was a symbol of classic modern art and architecture for Chicago, with its Brancusi bird announcing arrival to Mies van der Rohe's only interior space. It was like a flower springing from the ground-floor entrance, with the stair as its stem and the fluid space of the galleries, dining room, and lounge as the blossom. In spite of its two-story stair, the Mies space was meant to be perceived as a continuous horizontal space. The flow, modulation, and precision of its edges could not have existed had any hierarchy been established by the stairs. The height was consciously denied by the minimal opening that modulated the prelude to the ascent to the Arts Club. This was its history but unfortunately not its future. The great interior was destined to be a victim of the wrecking ball.

The club sold the Brancusi to raise funds for a new home. A site a block and a half east was purchased and an architectural competition was initiated by the club, whose membership is nearly one-third architects. The committee stated that it wanted to create a club for the twenty-first century, **reinforcing its dedication to the avant-garde.**

Our design insists that the two-story solution be read as a whole, as was Mies's original. A fluid space is compressed to the edges of the overlapping rectangles, tightly integrating the space vertically as well as horizontally. Our intention is clear even from the initial reading of the proposed corners, which have monolithic two-story walls. The interior compositions break down and layer the two-story space. In this design the courtyard creates a rectangle that is isolated and too dominant. It was necessary to neutralize and decentralize this element, to invert the space so that it would flow to the perimeter. This achieves a harmonious and integrated space that completes the original rectangle. The building was then raised on a platform to separate the club from the street and simultaneously to initiate the entrance sequence.

The functional requirements are simple. Reception and major galleries with back-up areas are located on the ground floor. On the second floor are a lounge, which could be used for informal lectures or stage productions, and a major dining area with appropriate services. Underlying the conception of each solution was the abstract function of flexibility, which would insist upon the integration of the rectangles **and the elegant flow of space.**

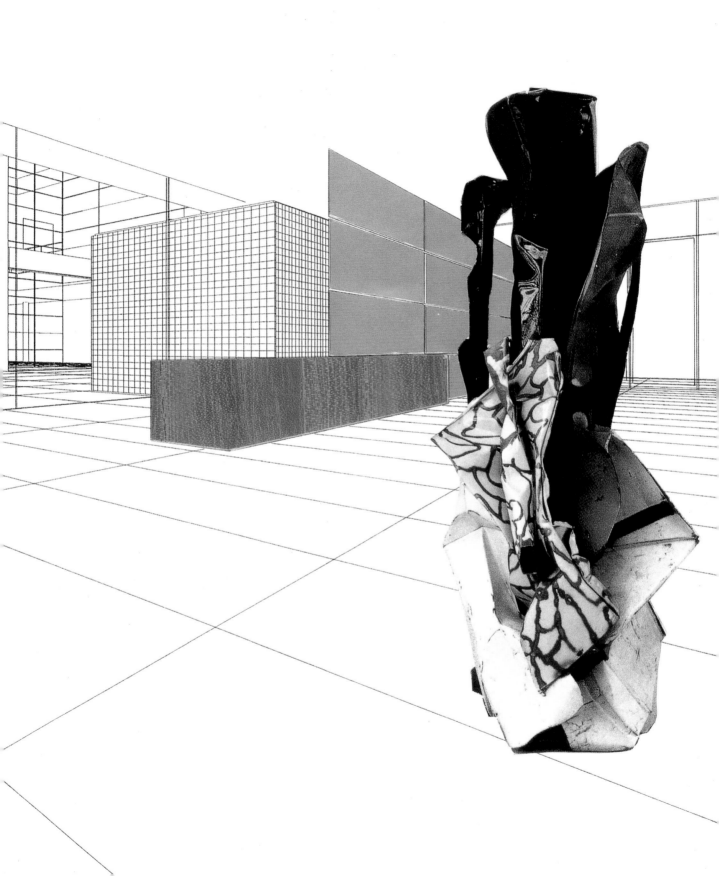

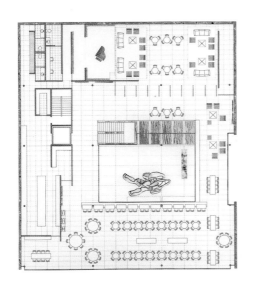

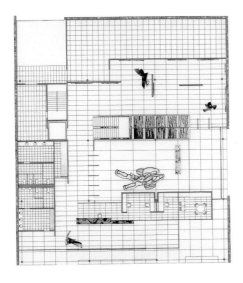

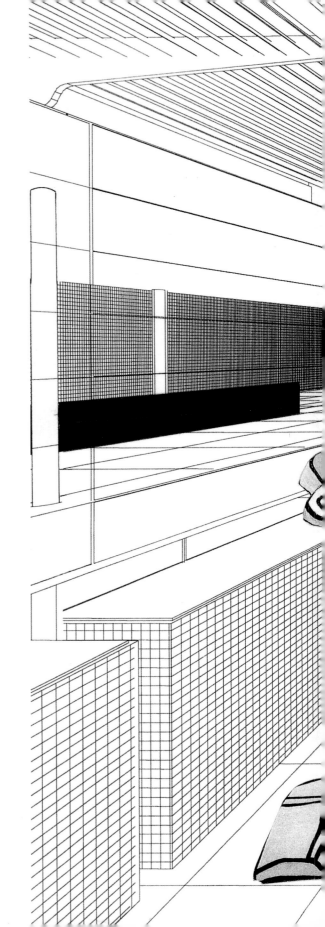

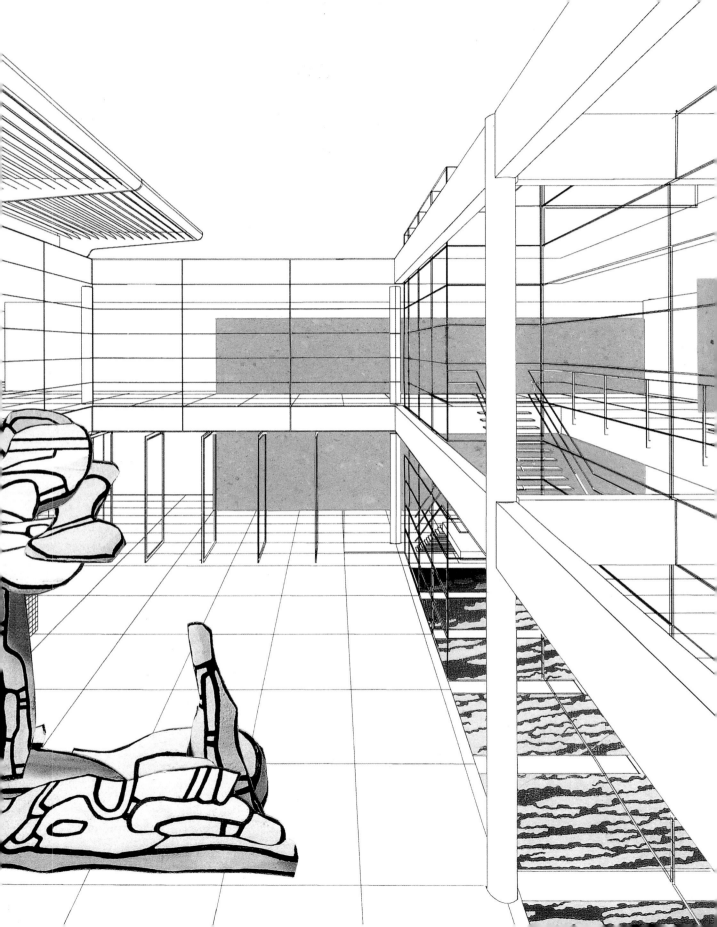

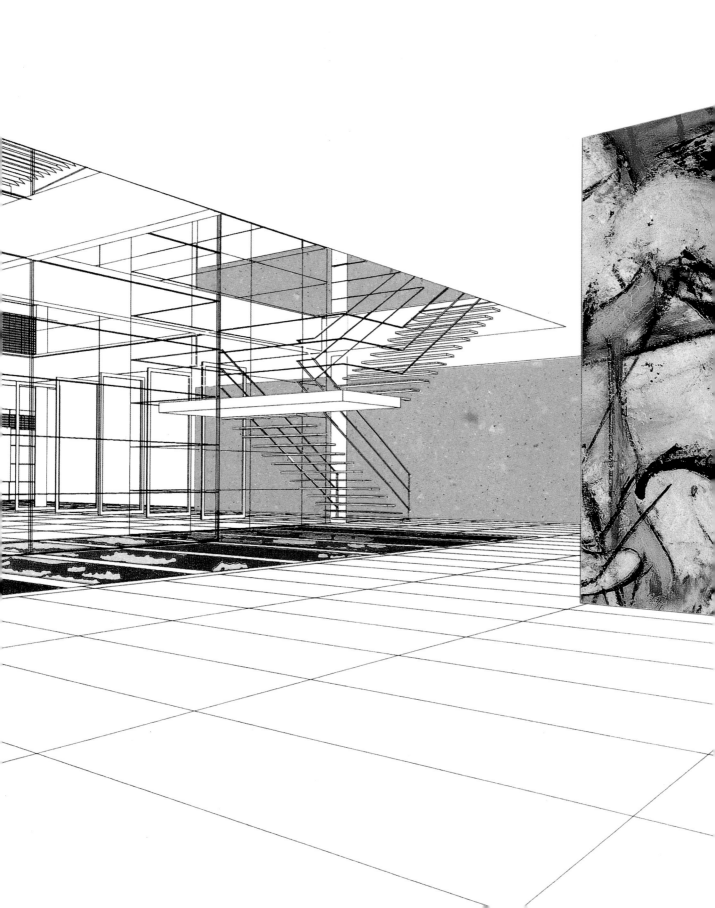

Chronology of Works

PROJECTS ARE ARRANGED ACCORDING TO FINISH DATE

1981

A Steel and Glass House
CHICAGO

1982

Thonet Showroom
CHICAGO

1983

The Painted Apartment
CHICAGO

Joseph Cornell Galleries
THE ART INSTITUTE OF CHICAGO

Dart Gallery
CHICAGO

1984

Hartmarx Corporation Corporate Offices
CHICAGO

1985

Runnion Residence
CHICAGO

A Victorian Townhouse Extended
CHICAGO

1986

Bannockburn Lake Office Plaza
BANNOCKBURN, ILLINOIS

Schal Associates Corporate Offices
CHICAGO

Untitled No. 3
CHICAGO

1987

Untitled No. 1
CHICAGO

1988

Amerika-Gedenkbibliothek
(American Library in Berlin) PROJECT

Hewitt Associates Corporate Headquarters
LINCOLNSHIRE, ILLINOIS

McConnaughy Stein Schmidt Brown Offices
CHICAGO

Untitled No. 2
CHICAGO

Frank C. Nahser Advertising Offices
CHICAGO

Stone Residence
CHICAGO

Untitled No. 4 PROJECT
CHICAGO

1989

Chemical Bank Offices
CHICAGO

The Chicago Christian Industrial League Campus Plan

Combustion Engineering Offices
CHICAGO

Dow Jones / Telerate Offices
CHICAGO

Hewitt Associates Eastern Regional Center
ROWAYTON, CONNECTICUT

1990

Crown Home Furnishings Offices and Showrooms
NEW YORK

Marketing Corporation of America /
Lee Hill Corporation Offices
CHICAGO

Peck Residence
CHICAGO

Peck Residence
PALM SPRINGS

1991

D'Alba Residence PROJECT
HIGHLAND PARK, ILLINOIS

1992

Cochrane Residence
CHICAGO

The Stainless Steel Apartment
CHICAGO

Northern Trust Company Investment Center
TORONTO

1993

Herman Miller Showrooms
CHICAGO

Northern Trust Company of California Bank
LOS ANGELES

Northern Trust Company of California Corporate Offices
LOS ANGELES

Silverman Residence
CHICAGO

1994

Hart Schaffner and Marx Factory Consolidation
DES PLAINES, ILLINOIS

Northern Trust Company of California Bank
NEWPORT BEACH

Northern Trust Company of California Bank
CENTER WEST

1995

The Arts Club of Chicago PROJECT

William Switzer and Associates Showrooms
CHICAGO

1996

Arian, Lowe and Travis Offices
CHICAGO

Museum of Science and Industry Feasibility Study
CHICAGO

Illinois Institute of Technology Feasibility Study
CHICAGO

First of America Bank Feasibility Study
CHICAGO

Western Textile Corporate Offices
DEERFIELD, ILLINOIS

A Brick and Glass House
CHICAGO

For projects completed prior to 1991, the architect of record is Krueck & Olsen Architects.

1994

Renaissance Society,
Turn of the Century House, University of Chicago

American Institute of Architecture,
Chicago Chapter, Awards, Chicago Historical Society

1993

American Institute of Architecture,
Chicago Chapter, Awards, Chicago Historical Society

CHICAGO ARCHITECTURE AND DESIGN, 1923–1993
Art Institute of Chicago

1991

G201 Gallery, Kent State University

1990

THE CHICAGO VILLA
Chicago Athenaeum

1989

NEW YORK ARCHITECTURE
German Museum of Architecture, Frankfurt
(exhibition traveled to Vienna, Madrid, Seville, and Taipei)

Archithese, Switzerland

ARQUITECTURA DE CHICAGO
Portugal

1987

EMERGING GENERATION IN THE U.S.A.
GA Gallery, Tokyo

HOUSE/HOUSING
John Nichols Gallery, New York

Gensler Gallery, San Francisco

1986

40 UNDER 40
Interiors Magazine and the Architectural League
of New York, International Design Center/New York

1985

150 YEARS OF CHICAGO ARCHITECTURE
Museum of Science and Industry, Chicago

1983

EMERGING VOICES 1983
Architectural League of New York

1982

CHICAGO ARCHITECTS DESIGN
Art Institute of Chicago

1981–82

Galleria D'Arte Moderna, Rome

1981

NEW CHICAGO ARCHITECTURE
Museo di Castelvecchio, Verona

1996

HONOR AWARD
American Institute of Architects, Chicago Chapter

1995

FIRST PLACE
BANK FOR NORTHERN TRUST COMPANY OF CALIFORNIA
Architecture and Design Society of the
Art Institute of Chicago

1994

CERTIFICATE OF MERIT
American Institute of Architects, Chicago Chapter

1993

INTERIOR DESIGN HALL OF FAME

CERTIFICATE OF MERIT
American Institute of Architects, Chicago Chapter

1988

DISTINGUISHED BUILDING HONOR AWARD
American Institute of Architects, Chicago Chapter

NATIONAL ARCHITECTURAL DESIGN AWARD
Pittsburgh Corning, Glass-Block

1986

NATIONAL HONOR AWARD
American Institute of Architects

40 UNDER 40
Interiors Magazine and the Architectural League
of New York, International Design Center/New York

ENERGY CONSERVATION AWARD
ASHRAE, Illinois Chapter

1985

INTERIOR ARCHITECTURE CERTIFICATE OF MERIT
American Institute of Architects, Chicago Chapter

1984

INTERIOR ARCHITECTURE HONOR AWARD
American Institute of Architects, Chicago Chapter

DISTINGUISHED BUILDING AWARD
American Institute of Architects, Chicago Chapter

1981

HONOR AWARD
American Institute of Steel Construction

1980

DISTINGUISHED BUILDING AWARD
American Institute of Architects, Chicago Chapter

Selected Bibliography

1995

KENNETH FRAMPTON
American Masterworks
NEW YORK : RIZZOLI

ROBERT PACKARD AND BALTHAZAR KORAB
Encyclopedia of American Architecture
NEW YORK : MCGRAW/HILL

Interior Design
MARCH

1994

Architecture + Urbanism (JAPAN)
MAY

Interior Design
JULY

1993

GA Houses 40 (JAPAN)

Progressive Architecture
MAY

Casabella (ITALY)
DECEMBER

1990

Quaderns 184 (SPAIN)

Ambiente (GERMANY)
FEBRUARY

Hauser (GERMANY)
FEBRUARY

Casa Vogue (SPAIN)
APRIL

Interior Design
MAY

1989

Architectural Record
FEBRUARY

Ambiente (GERMANY)
JUNE

Progressive Architecture
NOVEMBER

1988

Global Architecture 24 (JAPAN)

New York Times, Arts Section
JULY 7

Architectural Record
SEPTEMBER

Amerika-Gedenkbibliotheck (BERLIN)
NOVEMBER

1987

Global Architecture: Houses (JAPAN)

Abitare (ITALY)
JULY

Progressive Architecture
DECEMBER

1986

Forum (HOLLAND)
MARCH

Architecture + Urbanism (JAPAN)
AUGUST

Architectural Record
SEPTEMBER

Domus (ITALY)
SEPTEMBER

Interiors
SEPTEMBER

1985

Global Architecture 17 (JAPAN)

Interiors
AUGUST

1984

House & Garden
MARCH

Toshi-Jukatu (JAPAN)
MARCH

Ambiente (GERMANY)
APRIL

Chicago Magazine
DECEMBER

1983

Progressive Architecture
AUGUST

Architectural Record
SEPTEMBER

Nikkei Architecture (JAPAN)
DECEMBER

1982

Global Architecture 12 (JAPAN)

Casa Vogue (SPAIN)
AUGUST

1981

Progressive Architecture
DECEMBER

1980

Inland Architect
SEPTEMBER

Photography Credits
NUMBERS REFER TO PAGE NUMBERS

Richard Bryant
65, 66, 74, 75

Yukio Futagawa
68, 69, 70, 71, 72, 73

Bill Hedrich/Hedrich Blessing
20–21, 22–23, 25, 28, 32–33

Sandy Hedrich/Hedrich Blessing
87, 89

Timothy Hursley/The Arkansas Office
27, 30–31, 41, 48, 49, 50–51, 53, 56–57,
59, 60, 61, 62–63, 97, 101

Marco Lorenzetti/Hedrich Blessing
103, 106, 107, 121, 123, 128–29, 133, 137,
138, 139, 140, 141, 143, 144, 145, 146, 147,
148–49, 150, 151, 161, 164–65, 172–73,
175, 176–77, 184–85

Nick Merrick/Hedrich Blessing
35, 36, 38–39, 43, 44, 45, 46–47, 77, 80,
81, 82–83, 84, 85, 91, 92–93, 94, 95, 96,
98, 99, 105, 109, 110–11, 112, 113, 114,
115, 116–17, 118–19, 153, 154–55

Sadin-Karant
26

Paul Warchol
124–25, 126–27, 131, 132

DATE DUE

